W9-CKH-959

Eurydice's Song

Poem by
William Borden

Monotypes by
Douglas Kinsey

St. Andrews College Press
1700 Dogwood Mile
Laurinburg, North Carolina 28352

Text Copyright © 1999 by William Borden
Art Copyright © 1999 by Douglas Kinsey

Published by:

St. Andrews College Press
1700 Dogwood Mile
Laurinburg, North Carolina 28352

Design by Rachel Hershfield/RH Design

Typeset in Goudy OldStyle

Library of Congress Cataloging-in-Publication Data

Borden, William. Eurydice's song / William Borden
Kinsey Douglas. Eurydice's song / Douglas Kinsey
Laurinburg, NC / St. Andrews College Press
I. Borden, William. II. Kinsey, Douglas. III. Title

ISBN: 1-879934-58-2

First Printing: August 1999

For Marjorie Kinsey and Nancy Lee-Borden

"Eurydice!"
              you cry, your bare
feet slapping the rocky floor,
your steps uncertain, as if
the journey here were tricky,
the destination secret, the soul's
sure home unknown.
                  What
took you so long? I
disappeared
           months ago.

You call
again, "Eurydice! Eurydice!"
yearning, afraid, your
boyish cry an echoing
animal bleat, as if scenting blood
from a slaughter house.

"I'm here!" I cry.

My voice flutters
against the stony walls
like the wings of tiny bats.

You will expect me
to be grateful.

There was no snake.
No abduction.
No swift carrying-off.

It was the dark that seduced me. Hades'
deep eyes, black beard, heavy voice. A figure
blacker than the night, as if there were a vacancy
in the order of things,
                        a bear-like man, sitting
by gaping rocks: a path leading down, a womb
to walk into, a dangerous safety, a violent solace.

He held out his hand. His palm
was all shadow. There was no future
there for the fortune-tellers to read.
But I knew what future lay in that hand.

His body seemed to sink into the earth.
Only his hand remained, open, waiting.
My fingers lost themselves
in his thick, hot palm, a calloused
farmer's hand, it seemed.

It was like sinking thankfully
into a soothing pool of night's warm water.

I entered that darkness
willingly.
                        You
were nowhere around.

And so you've come for me,
dressed up, suited out, high-stepping,
flute and lyre hanging from your belt—
you think you're pretty hot.

Were you desperate
for me? Or merely bored? Winter's snows
kept you warmer than my breasts? Ice
caressed your smooth skin, sleet kissed
those lips puffed from fluting?

Or did other arms
wrap your loneliness in a forgetfulness
more poignant than despair?

Was it love that brought you here? The anguish
of absence? Or curiosity
and your hurly burly pride that dares
everything? This was the tune
no one had played, this journey to the dark.

I was your excuse, not your beloved.

                                                You
were afraid I had forgotten you?
Oh, no, my smooth-cheeked boy.

                                                You made
the trees waltz. Birds slowed their swift flights
to glide atop your rhythms. I could hold
a stone to my ear, and the stone sang.

                                                  Your
melodies perfumed the breeze with hyacinths,
high notes tickled the soles of my feet.

                                                      I danced
with the others, behind you, up hillsides and down,
our bare feet crushing wild thyme,
through forests curtained by brambles and nettles, over
sharp blades of volcanic rock,
                                        into storms
racked by thunder where lightning played

like the legs of dancers gone berserk.
Blood and pain were counterpoints, forgetfulness
a fugue. We chased oblivion.
                              Our naked
feet drummed desire. Percussion drowned
all reason. We couldn't tell ourselves
from one another, were caught in a communion so sweet
it was an exquisite agony,
while the fragrance of thyme
                              steamed from our skin
like reflected moonlight
                              and desperate love.

They danced to lose themselves.
I danced to find myself.

You pushed aside handsome young men,
elbowed gray-haired matrons, ignored
skinny naiads, stepped over thick-thighed
married women lounging in the grass
to fall at my side
                    where we lay
on poppies and anemones.

                        Your song
was quiet as grass growing, your fingers slippery
as stones in a stream, your kisses soft as asphodels.
You thrummed my skin's secret melody, my heels
rattled earth's tight skin, my breasts
rose to meet your longing, my trembling thighs
caught your teasing music, held it tight.

After you made love to me, when you thought
I was asleep, I watched you with the
large-breasted women, the soft young men,
arms and legs wrapped like vines of dark
ivy.

       Moonlight skinned your passion. Animal
growls rasped from your throats.

                You were a flute,
played by anyone who put you
           to her lips.

                                        I've been
all right. Well taken care of. The center
of attention, really.

                        He sits at my feet,
prefers me to music.

He says it was the flowery scent of my breath,
the softness of my hair, the perfect shape
of my hands, the press of my small feet against
the earth that drew him, alone, without
his retinue, to climb that rocky passageway
so far from the safe hollows of his world,
from peaceful night to raucous life,
a quickening he was fearful of.
                                    He could feel,
he said, the warm indentation as my body
lay resting on the soft earth, feel
the grass's bending, the small push of my breathing,
the troubled drumming of my heart. He ran

to find me.

It's easy to get here, to this gritty
infinity that seems so crowded,
this afterthought of life, nightmare
and relief in one last breath.

The stories you've heard—three-headed dogs,
rivers, boatmen, traps, tests, bogs—
are the fiery imaginings of topside poets:
scare tactics to hold an audience.

He welcomes you graciously, without jealousy,
as he welcomed Odysseus, when he came,
briefly. We have many callers who peer
into the shadows, then walk away.

You found your way when you leaped
into the emptiness in your heart?

We've heard you playing. Your music hums through earth
and rock until you seem to be here
with us.
   So you see, your coming is not so special.
Oh, your notes are clearer, your vibrato more
reckless. We hear the squeak of your fingers across
the strings, the intake of breath before the song.
But we've heard music before. We're not without
our own musicians. We're not country bumpkins.

It's not lonely down here. Nor frightening.
It's like belonging to a family. We're a democracy
of shadows. It's difficult to explain,
my fine, proud, handsome prince.

Here time embraces us like an old lover.
Day and night are one.
An hourglass drops a grain of sand
so slowly we count its fall in breaths.

We make no plans. Have no regrets.
No guilt. We abandon expectation.
Nothing surprises us.
I don't know why, Orpheus.
It's just that we're content.

Do you think I've been pining for you?

Now that you're here,
                Orpheus,
my daring rescuer,
                    you strum complaining dirges,
flute uncertain threnodies, not
the pounding frenzies of your moon-stirred concerts.

You miss noon's eye-squinting dance,
drumming that rattles the whitewashed houses,
winter's snow-muffled silence, the blood-red
poppies carousing in spring, the aspen leaves
rustling like fingers tapping on the breeze?

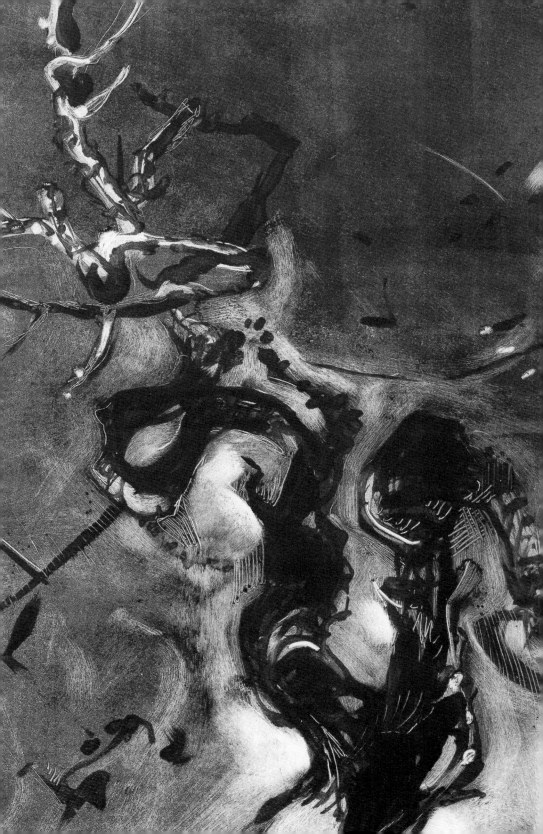

Other voices sing you. Their
ecstasy fires yours. This
is the key to your charm. This
is the secret of your music.

Bereft of your adoring ones, you wither
like a leaf in autumn, grow shadowy,
a misty memory. You feed on others'
raptures. You're starving here.

You're moody, sullen, bored.
You pace. You climb the rocks.
Your impatience ripples through our calm,
your headlong strolls plow a wake of turmoil.
You vanish into our labyrinths of indifference.

Do you want to leave me? Or save me?

I wrap my warm arms around Hades'
hairy chest. We make love in lamplight.
Shadows heave across the wall.

Are you watching, Orpheus?

Do you like to watch?

I've been more reckless, wilder, more passionate
with Hades since you've come.

Have you noticed?

I smell thyme, crushed on a rocky hillside,
in my hair, on my breath, a constant perfume.

You could stay, you know.

Would I have the best of both worlds?

Or only shadows?

You could stay.

Hades? Quite the gentleman.
                              "Anything
you want, old boy. Stay as long
as you like. Leave when the mood strikes.
                                        Eurydice?
Could have left
                    anytime.
Could leave now.
                        She knows the way. There's
one entrance. No doors, gates, locks.
That's it."

You don't believe him. You say,
                              "There must
be a trick."

                    "You want a trick?"
                                        Hades asks.

You say you know there is one.

                              "I can see,"
he says, "you're a man who plunges ahead. Never
looks back."

                    "That's me," you say.

                                    "That's
the trick," Hades says. "Be yourself.
                              Don't look back."

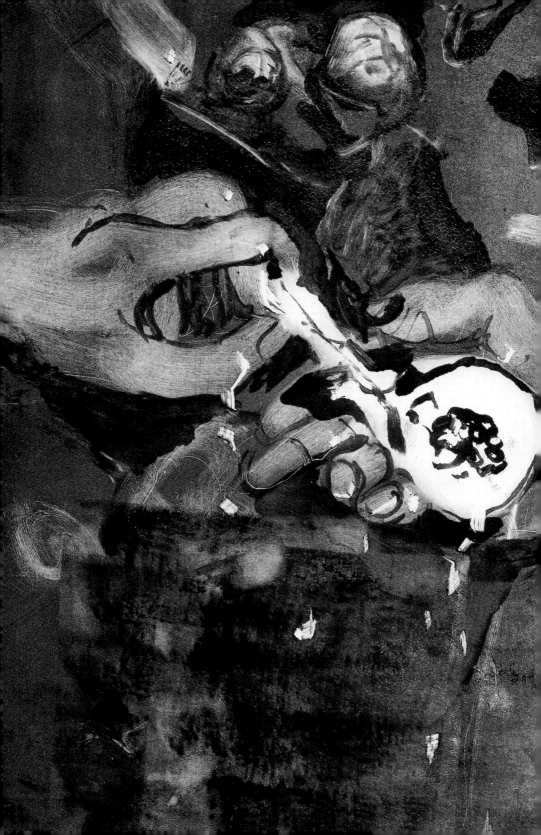

I remember one bright day
we plucked fresh figs from gnarled trees
beside stone walls. Our fingers tore
at the ripe fruit. Seeds like tiny teeth
popped from the scarlet pulp, juice dripped
from our fingers, sticky as memory.

We kiss. I hold your head
in my hands, my palms against
the throbbing in your throat.
My fingers curl around your ears,
forbidding you to hear.

Your head belongs to me.
The rest is theirs.

"Follow me," you say, sure of your way.
But I clutch your arm, my fingers gripping
your hot flesh, your eagerness
a blood-frothed river poised
to plunge into catastrophe.

                                    You lunge
from my grasp, this timeless cold certainty
no match for the frantic change of seasons, days,
climate, mood.
                        I don't move. I
watch you lope up the corridor,
the glow of torches warming your impatient
shoulders, until you dissolve into the dusk
of long travel. Then I begin walking.

And why should you look back?
                                    You
were followed everywhere. Everyone
adored you. Long trains of devotees
wound through woods, over hills,
across streams. Men, women, children,
birds, butterflies, wolves, snakes,
wildcats leaped, flew, writhed in your wake.
Old oaks lunged after you,
their gnarled roots quaking in the earth,
straining for release, desiring uprooting,
wanting nothing more than to follow.

                                    Who
could not follow you?

Pebbles, torn from the rocky floor by your quick
feet, skitter against my ankles. The path
steepens. You run as if to lose me.

Dark corridors twist like despair,
your frantic footsteps fade into the distance,
breath catches at my throat, pain grabs
my ribs, a rock bounces off the wall.
I stumble, my fingers slip along wet adamant,
my knees scrape the floor. I scramble
up, climb, listen for the ricocheting stones,
no singing now, or fluting, to lead me
to some bright destiny.

                   I turn
a corner. I see your shadowed head,
your thrusting legs, the sweat filming your back.

Sunlight spills across the dark passage.

You run headlong into brilliance.

Will you leave without me? Burst
into that sunny freedom alone,
forgetting me
               again?

                    Without thinking,

my panicked heart cries out—
                       "Orpheus!"

You turn.

Our eyes meet like lovers' eyes, soft,
knowing, seeing everything in an instant.

For a moment we imagine we have escaped,
are safe.
               Then we recognize each other
for the first time.
                  The space between us,
heavy with understanding, is a space too
sudden for recrimination.
               You step
backwards, one foot, another,
into a brilliant shimmering.

               You are
a shadow emblazoned by fire, drawn into air,
sucked by life's mutability
               into absence.

Suddenly, from that other world
of flowers and rain and uncertainties,
cheers erupt like loneliness
exploding, and cries of victory clamor,
reverberate down these rocks,
ring in my ears loud as heartbreak.

I sink to the hard floor, cold, shivering.

The light fades, as if clouds were rushing into thunder.

Later, you loll about in lazy abandon,
you and the plump-breasted women, their hair
wild and long, their lids heavy, their throats
hoarse from singing. It is evening.

                                  You
brag, Yes, you were down there,
deep in the bedrock of fear, where
it's darker than the center of the mind.

You say, it's like a dream now, blurred
by sunlight and intolerable regret. You say,
perhaps the voices you heard down there
were only in your head. Perhaps,
you say, that's what death is—
ourselves speaking to ourselves.

You begin to sing, perhaps to someone
who isn't there, as if that yearning
could fill an emptiness too deep,
a solitude too rending to name.

It seems to the caressing women
to be an emptiness they can fill
if only they can reach it.

They kiss you all over your body,
as if they are playing a flute, their pouting
lips full, wet, thirsty, hungry.

Their kisses grow teeth.
They nibble love bites.
You twist away, teasing their hunger.
The distance between their skins and yours
gnaws at their impatience. You lunge
into their white teeth, desperate
to remember everything. The women
gorge on your grief. Their nails
dig deeper, searching for the wound
that gives your music such lonely purity.

When you croon,
                    "Eurydice!"
                                        "Eurydice!"

the women, maddened by ravenous love,
wanting to be you, become you,
enter you, tear arm from shoulder,
leg from hip, gut with teeth and rending
hands your belly, eat greedily,
chew your throbbing heart. Blood
spills across their naked breasts. They
smile. They laugh. They never blink.
Their breath comes fast. Their bare feet
lightly touch the crimson earth.

Yet still you sing, from bloody lips,
as if your keening melody would
bring me to you, as if I could save you
even now, while the adoring women,
abandoned by the song that's not for them,
twist and wrench your singing head
free with bloody fingers, toss
it, singing, back and forth,
awed and wanting to keep it but afraid
to feel those moving lips so cold,
the tongue so agile, and they finally hurl it,
calling my name, into the dancing river,
where it sings yet, riding the rolling
foam to the blue cold sea.

Later, they remember the song you
were singing, the name you were
calling. They say, "He loved so many
of us.

                   Was she so special?"

Now, down here in the night thoughts
of the soul, we believe we can
hear you still, your clear, full
voice caught in the rocky walls,

your playful plucking of the lute resonant
in the air, the celestial wail of your flute
lingering in our ears, humming from the boulders
on which we lounge, timeless, silent, listening.